TALL SHIPS 1986

by
Cy and Pat Liberman

The Middle Atlantic Press
Wilmington, Delaware 19899

TALL SHIPS 1986

A MIDDLE ATLANTIC PRESS BOOK

Copyright © 1986 by Cy and Pat Liberman

First Middle Atlantic Press printing, June 1986

The Middle Atlantic Press, Inc.
848 Church Street, P.O. Box 945
Wilmington, Delaware 19899
ISBN: 0-912608-29-3

Designed by Emre Kavlakoglu

Printed in Spain by Printer I.G.S.A. Barcelona

Table of Contents

Publisher's Note

This souvenir edition of Tall Ships will be followed by a deluxe hardbound edition with the same title containing additional information on ship preservation, restored ships, museums and seaports, the history of sail and ship models.

To be placed on the list for notification when the hardback book is available, please write to:

Middle Atlantic Press
848 Church Street
P.O. Box 945
Wilmington, Delaware 19899

Middle Atlantic Press also publishes *The Mid-Atlantic Treasure Coast*, by Stephen M. Voynick, *The Crab Book*, by Cy and Pat Liberman, *Blackbeard the Pirate and Other Stories of the Pine Barrens*, by Larona Homer, *The Jersey Devil*, by James F. McCloy and Ray Miller, Jr., and many other fascinating books about the Middle Atlantic region.

For orders and information, write Middle Atlantic Press at the above address.

Acknowledgments

We are grateful to many generous people for valuable assistance in producing this book. Stanley Budner originated the idea. Experts in maritime history, building replicas, and sail training, as well as Tall Ships buffs with remarkable libraries, shared information with us. These include Peter Stanford of the National Maritime Historical Society, Norman Brouwer of South Street Seaport, Melbourne Smith of the International Historical Watercraft Society, Captain George Crowninshield of the American Sail Training Association, and Bernie Klay of Sea Heritage Foundation. Donald W. Callender Jr., John Dossett, Captain Charles M. Quinlan, E.I. duPont de Nemours & Co., the Granger Collection, Malcolm MacKenzie, Albert Cizauskas, Jr. and others provided photographs. We thank Thomas E. Miller and Pamela Hoffman for translation, Shari Gallagher-Phalan for typing, and Joan Ware Colgan for research.

In any compilation of facts and figures of this magnitude, there is a high probability of imperfection. Any errors that turn up are strictly our own responsibility and we trust will be reported for correction later.

C. & P. L.

Preface

Everyone enjoys the beauty and majesty of Tall Ships. The evidence is the swarming masses of people who crowd the waterfronts and pepper the waterways with boats whenever there is an opportunity to see the Tall Ships. The purpose of this book is to add to that enjoyment by supplying ship-watchers with pertinent background to enlarge the picture they are seeing. Here they will find facts on individual ships and the roles they play today, as well as the history of Tall Ships and their part in the development of the civilized world. In addition, there are details on the design and rigging of different types of sailing vessels of the past and present.

The ship-watcher, after reading this book, will not only be able to identify the ships as they sail past, but he or she will enjoy them again and again in memory with the help of the illustrations.

The grand dames of the Tall Ships are the school ships—the largest sailing vessels in active use today. They are gorgeous reminders of the fleets of sailing vessels that transported humans and their cargo on all the oceans of the world before the advent of steamships and aircraft. Those great ships are few in number now, but with their ballooning clouds of square-rigged sails, they are perhaps the most fascinating of all sailing craft to observe.

There is also tremendous interest in the larger schooners and other yachts—all billowing beauties on the water as they gather the breeze and bend it to their purposes in one of the most challenging and invigorating of human endeavors, the art of sailing.

The Mystique of Tall Ships

The ability of humans of ancient times to create, without our advanced technology, objects of beauty and utility is a source of wonder to thoughtful people today. We view with amazement the feat of the Egyptians in building the pyramids thousands of years ago without a crane to lift those mammoth blocks of rock. Ancient Greeks shaped stones into handsome buildings and splendid sculpture. Through the ages and throughout the world, a vast array of human creations have combined art and technical skill in ways that modern people look upon with awe. Not the least of these inspired creations are ships.

On our own continent, most Americans have a deep admiration and a kind of patriotic pride in the record of the early settlers from Europe who used the axe so skillfully to cut their way through the wilderness, then used the adze so masterfully to transform those trees into ships. We marvel at their resourcefulness and craftmanship. These are important elements in the mystique of Tall Ships.

Beyond the beauty of clouds of set sails, beyond the bewildering maze of rigging, another element in the enchantment of the Tall Ships is a linkage we feel with our past. Wherever our immigrant ancestors came from, many came by sail, and we feel a reverence for our roots as symbolized by the square-rigged ships we see at seaport museums or coastal celebrations.

That many of our forbears came here, some in chains, most in miserably overloaded, insubstantial ships, awash with disease and constant discomfort, contributes to the mystique, and history comes alive. One can look up at the mighty yards, the highflung sails and picture "the flung spray, the blown spume, the seagulls flying" and hear "the wind's song and the white sail's shaking" of Masefield's evocative poem. Whatever reason our ancestors had for coming across to these shores, that romance and adventure is expressed today in our affection for Tall Ships.

Add to this our love of the sea—conscious and subconcious. Some of us are all but hypnotized by looking at the sea, watching the endless motion of the waves and swells. Others are drawn to go upon the sea in boats and ships of all kinds—anything that will float and let an individual feel surrounded by and close to the water, out on a small part of an immense pathway that connects all corners of the earth. We know the Tall Ships could go anywhere on that broad pathway, driven by the wind alone in some half understood and half mysterious way.

To many who love the sea and also love small boats, the sheer size and strange rigging on the old sailing ships are matters of wonder. A 72-foot ketch seems impressively large. But a schooner twice as long and a bark three or four times as long are matters for amazement. We love sailing boats. We are in awe of sailing ships.

We are no less affected by the materials used in the construction of these vessels. At home with modern fiberglass, aluminum and wood of a modest thickness, citizens of the 20th Century are often overwhelmed by the weight of the iron, steel and timbers in the frames and planks of old ships. Can a hull that heavy really sail? Obviously, they not only sailed—they circumnavigated our earth!

And then we look at the rigs. How could those oldtime skippers get where they wanted to go with square sails? Clearly, they mastered the prevailing winds and currents, applied the sailing lore of generations, and forced those rigs to carry them to their far away destinations and back. The more we know about boats of our own time, the more we marvel at the ships of an earlier era and the men who sailed them.

All those strands and perhaps many more are woven into the fabric of emotion that constitutes the mystique of the Tall Ships.

How Tall Is Tall?

How to Identify Tall Ships

What do people mean when they speak of the Tall Ships?

They usually mean the square-riggers and other large sailing vessels—all those watercraft that are like swans among a flock of ducks. This book is about both—the square-rigged ships that are the stars of all gatherings of Tall Ships and the big schooners and other larger-than-ordinary yachts that are featured players at those gatherings.

These ships are fairly rare. People rush to see them when the opportunities arise, all too infrequently.

Not only are viewers thrilled at the sight of the Tall Ships, but they find it a pleasant sport to identify them by rig and look up their dimensions. The material in the following pages provides easy-to-understand guidelines and dimensions.

This book does not place the Tall Ships in classes, nor does it rate them. They all deserve Class 1-A, four stars and gold medals.

One dimension given needs some explanation—the length overall of many vessels. It may be interpreted several ways. The legal definition of "overall length" excludes bowsprits and other attachments to the hull. Most Tall Ships do have bowsprits, however, and it is pertinent to know how long the ships are, including all projections. Technically that figure is known as "sparred length." Owners frequently report it as overall length.

The term "sparred length" is sometimes used in this book, but other terms such as "length overall" or simply "length" are also used. Unless "length on deck" is specified, the only length figure used here is sparred length. Put simply, if you were putting a Tall Ship alongside a pier, that is how much space it would require.

Once again, a Tall Ship is any large sailing vessel, square-rigged or not, and any square-rigged vessel regardless of size.

And finally, how large is large? How tall is tall? One need not draw an arbitrary line. Instead, the descriptions in these pages include the more interesting and unusual ships that shipwatchers sometimes have opportunities to see.

The smaller yachts that can be seen by the hundreds in any popular harbor are not listed.

The Types of Ships

Part of the fun of seeing Tall Ships is in being able to identify them. It is the same thing with stars, birds and flowers. One enjoys being able to say, "There's Orion's belt," or, "Look at that male goldfinch," or, "Here's a bloodroot."

To identify ships, the first step is to know the rig. Many of the larger, sail-training vessels in use today are *barks* (also spelled *barques*), *full-rigged ships* or *barkentines* and *brigantines*. *The difference are in the number of masts they have and kinds of sails on those masts.

Does the ship have at least one mast that has nothing on it but square sails? If the answer is yes, the next step is to count the number of masts. If the vessel has three or more masts, she must be a *bark,* a full-rigged ship or a barkentine. If she has only two masts, she must be a brigantine or a *brig.*

The next step in any identification process is to see where the square sails are, and, after we understand the difference, where any fore-and-aft sails are. Square sails are sometimes fairly square but are more often rectangular. They are held aloft on *yards,* which are horizontal *spars* attached to the mast. Square sails and their yards in normal position are aligned with the width of the ship, whereas fore-and-aft sails, as the term implies, are aligned with the ship's length.

Nautical terms italicized when first used are defined in the Glossary.

Brigantine

Brig

Gaff Rigged Sloop

Topsail Schooner

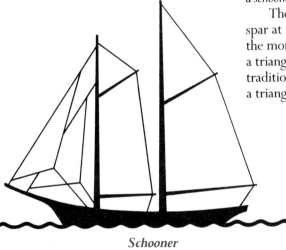

Schooner

They are the kind of sails we see on modern sailboats, small and large—sails which, when relaxed, follow the centerline of the boat from bow to stern. These include large sails attached to the aft side of the mast and to a *boom*—a *spar* at the bottom of the sail. Suppose you are standing at the waterfront watching a parade of Tall Ships, and one comes along. You count the masts; she has three. You look at the rigging-aha! There are square sails on all three masts—that vessel is a full-rigged ship. Perhaps she is *Amerigo Vespucci, Christian Radich,* or *Libertad.* You can tell by the national flag or ensign, or you may be able to read the name with the help of binoculars.

As the ship goes by, check to see if she has a small fore-and-aft sail on her last mast, called the *mizzen.* She may have, but if she also has square sails on that mast, she is still considered a full-rigged ship. However if she has no square sails on the mizzen, and has fore-and-aft sails there, she is a *bark* like *Eagle, Mircea* or *Sagres II.* Along comes another three-masted vessel. This one has square sails on the first mast only; without a doubt she is a barkentine such as *Palinuro,* or *Gazela of Philadelphia.* A very large ship with four masts, square-rigged on only the first, would probably be *Esmeralda,* the largest sail-training ship in the Western Hemisphere and a rare example of a four masted barkentine.

Remember that any three-masted vessel with square sails occupying all of one or more of her masts must be a full-rigged ship, a bark or a barkentine.

Among two masted vessels with square sails, the question is how to distinguish between a brig and a brigantine. If the ship is square-rigged on both her masts, she is a brig—a rather rare rig. The Indian Navy has a brig, *Varuna.*

If, on the other hand, the ship is square-rigged on the foremast only and has a fore-and-aft sail on her mainmast, she is a brigantine, like the new *Spirt of Chemainus.* A brigantine may or may not have a square sail above the fore-and-aft sail on her mainmast, which is the higher of the two masts.

Sometimes the term *hermaphrodite brig* is used: it means brigantine. The term was used long ago with the excuse that the rig is half that of a brig and half that of a *schooner.*

The fore-and-aft sail on the rigs just described is held up by a *gaff*—a slanting spar at the top of the sails. Such a sail is *gaff-rigged.* It has four sides in contrast to the more modern three-sided sails commonly used today. Gaff-rigged sails resemble a triangle with the top corner cut off diagonally. However, when you look at a traditional gaff-rigged sail with a smaller topsail over it, the two together look like a triangular sail in two parts, separated by the slanting gaff.

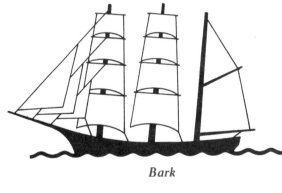

Bark

Barkentine

Fullrigged Ship

9

The same is true of the fore-and-aft sail at the stern of the bark or sometimes, of a full-rigged ship. That sail is called a *spanker,* and may be in two or three sections forming a triangle separated by one or two gaffs. The topmost section is called the *topsail* or *gaff topsail.* If a spanker is in two parts aside from the topsail, they are called the *upper and lower spanker.*

Does the Tall Ship you are watching have at least one mast that has nothing but square sails on it? If the answer is no, the ship is a fore-and-aft rigged vessel which may be one of at least seven types: *schooner, ketch, yawl, sloop, cutter, cat* or *lateen-rigged.*

The next step in this identification sport is to count the masts. If there are four and the ship is large, the vessel is a *schooner* and is probably *Juan Sebastian de Elcano,* one of the few large, four-masted schooners in existence. If there are three masts, the vessel is also a schooner. If there are two, she may be a schooner, a ketch, a yawl or a cat-ketch.

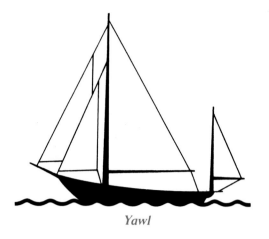

Yawl

Ketch

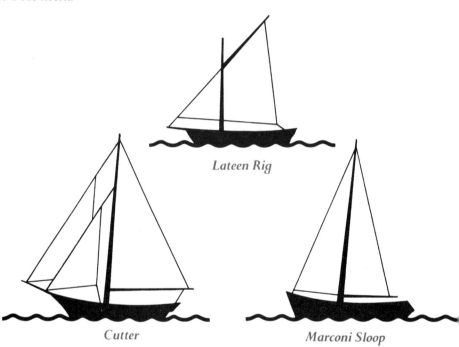

Lateen Rig

Cutter

Marconi Sloop

Next question: Which of the two masts is higher? If the second one is higher, the vessel is a schooner. The shorter one is called the *foremast* and the other is the *mainmast.*

Schooner Rig

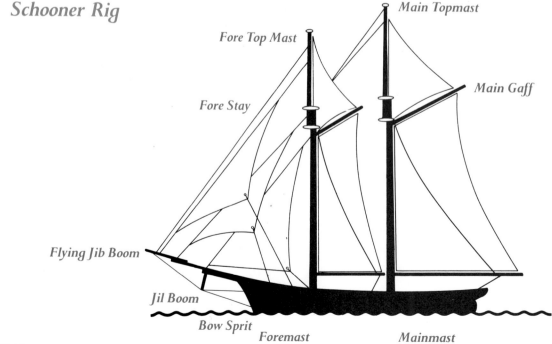

Fore Top Mast

Main Topmast

Fore Stay

Main Gaff

Flying Jib Boom

Jil Boom

Bow Sprit   *Foremast*   *Mainmast*

Many schooners have extra sails at the top of the mast and are dubbed *topsail schooners.* Those that have no topsail are sometimes called *bald.* At times, the topsails are square sails, as in the *Californian* and *Pride of Baltimore.* This does not make the ship a square-rigged vessel.

In addition to sails on their mainmast, most rigs described in this book have sails before the mainmast, called *staysails* or *jibs.* These are triangular sails set on a stay (usually a wire) between two masts or between a mast and the deck or the bowsprit.

When the stay runs from the foremast to the bowsprit, the staysail is similar to a jib and may be one of a series of sails supplementing one or more jibs.

Suppose the two-masted vessel has its higher mast forward. Then she is a *ketch* or *yawl* rather than a schooner. Each has a tall mainmast and a shorter mizzen or jiggermast further aft. On a yawl, the mizzenmast and its sail are smaller than on a ketch of similar size, but the technical difference is in the placement of the mast. In the yawl, the mast is aft of the rudderpost; in the ketch, it is forward of that post.

There is one more two-masted vessel that is easily recognized—the *cat-ketch.* In this rig, both masts are usually the same size. The foremast is far forward in the ship's bow and carries the mainsail. In many cat-ketches, the masts are unstayed (no fastening lines to the deck).

Schooner Sails

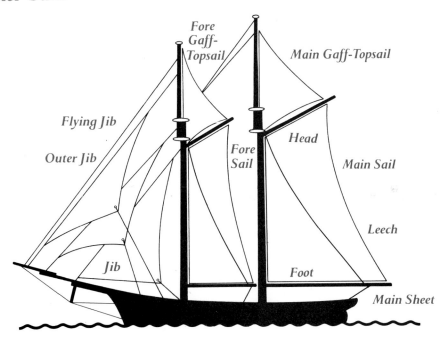

A ship with only one mast must be a *sloop,* a *cutter,* a *catboat,* or a *latten rigged* vessel. The sloop, in addition to the mainsail, normally has one working sail—a jib—forward of the mast, whereas the cutter has two—a jib and a staysail. Also, the cutter's mast is usually closer to the center of the boat. The sloop is the most popular rig on recreational sail boats today. Many sailors contend that the sloop rig is the most efficient for sailing upwind, and a high proportion of racing boats are sloop-rigged. The cat rig employs a single mast far forward in the ship, and a single sail, often gaff-rigged.

The lateen rig uses a triangular sail suspended from a long yard, set obliquely to the mast. Many Mediterranean and Nile River craft, and many from other parts of the world, past and present, are lateen-rigged. In the United States, it is seen on the popular Sunfish and other small recreational boats.

Square Sails

Each sail on a square-rigged ship, or any other sailing vessel, has a name. When the skipper orders crew members to furl the *main skysail,* there can be no doubt which sail he wants rolled up and secured. On a full-rigged ship or a bark, there are likely to be from 30 to 34 different sails, each with a name indicating which mast it is on as well as its position on that mast.

If the ship has six levels of square sails on the mainmast, the lowest and largest sail is called the *mainsail* (pronounced mayn'sl) or *main course.* Above the mainsail is the *main lower topsail* (pronounced tops'l), and over that flies the *main upper topsail.* At the fourth level up from the deck is the *main topgallant,* followed by the *main royal.* All the way at the top is the *top skysail* (pronounced skys'l).

Today's curious dockside observer may have a casual interest in knowing something about the sails and the running rigging of a square-rigged ship, but a brief brush with the marine vocabulary may be enough. Each sail and each yard has its own set of lines coming down to the deck in what is, to the uninitiated, an extremely complex array, like a gigantic spider web. Each line has its purpose in sailing the vessel and is fastened around its own *belaying pin.*

However, for the seaman working on a square-rigged ship in the old days, it was absolutely essential to "learn the ropes"–and quickly! Every crew member had to know all the lines and to be able to locate the right belaying pin for each line–in double quick time! To make sure seamen learned, it was customary for officers to devise complex drills that chased the seamen from bow to stern, locating pins as orders were shouted. Punishment, some outrageously cruel, was the lot of crew members who could not match line to belaying pin. The most inhuman punishment was the famous keel-haul, which meant tying the slow learner, throwing him overboard, dragging him under the vessel and up the other side.

The glossary of this book contains definitions of many of the terms used in identifying the sails and rigging, and supplements the illustrations. Informative displays on the rigging of square-rigged ships, showing the complexities of both the running rigging and standing rigging, which supports the masts, may be studied at the maritime museums.

The Ships

LIBERTAD
ARGENTINA

Her great size makes the full-rigged ship *Libertad* an impressive sight. She is 336 feet long and her rig towers 165 feet above the deck. The 2,587 ton vessel, with a draft of 23 feet and a beam of 45 feet, is owned by Argentina and is used as a training ship by that nation's navy. Built of steel, she was launched in 1959, and made her first voyage to Europe in 1963.

In 1966, and again in 1976, *Libertad* won medals for the distance she traveled in 24-hour runs, while trainees made up more than half her crew. In 1966, she sailed for 2,058 miles across the Atlantic from Canada to the Irish Sea in 8½ days.

Under full sail, *Libertad* flies five jibs on her long bowsprit.

Norman J. Brouwer

Norman J. Brouwer

ZENOBE GRAMME
BELGIUM

Belgium's contribution to the world of Tall Ships is a 92-foot ketch. This 149-ton vessel was commissioned in 1962. She has a beam of 22 feet, five inches and a draft of seven feet. Her mainmast is 95 feet tall; her 200 horsepower Diesel drives her at 10 knots. The ketch was designed for scientific research and carries a crew of 14.

ROBERTSON II
CANADA

An original Grand Banks fishing schooner, *Robertson II,* has a beam of 22 feet and a draft of 12 feet. She is a 98-ton wooden vessel, built in 1940 at Shelburne, Nova Scotia. (This is the same seacoast town where Donald McKay, famous designer and builder of clipper ships, was born.) *Robertson II* has 5,637 square feet of sail area and has a Diesel for auxiliary power. She is 130 feet long and her rig height is 109 feet.

Robertson II operates during the warm months as a sail-training vessel, taking 30 students on 10-day voyages for experience in shipboard life. She is worked by a crew of three.

This schooner is owned by the Sail and Life Training Society of Victoria, British Columbia, which also owns *Spirit of Chemainus.*

Malcolm Mackenzie

ESMERALDA
CHILE

With her overall length of 353 feet the four-masted barkentine, *Esmeralda*, is the largest sailing vessel in the Western Hemisphere, edging out *Libertad* for that honor, but bowing to *Kruzenstern* for the world title. *Esmeralda* is one of the most thrilling ships to see with her voluminous array of sails flying. She was built in 1952 at Cadiz, Spain, as a sister ship to that country's *Juan Sebastian de Elcano*, from which she differs only in rigging. Her original name was *Don Juan de Austria*, but before she was completely finished, she was destroyed by fire and sold in 1953 to Chile, where she was rebuilt and re-christened.

This barkentine is a huge, steel-hulled sailing ship, carrying 332 officers, crew and cadets. *Esmeralda* usually spends half of every year on training cruises for graduates of the Chilean Naval Academy. At her bow is a Condor, Chile's national bird, holding the nation's coat-of-arms in its claws. *Esmeralda's* beam is 44 feet, her draft 23 feet. Her mast height is 165 feet.

Fast under sail or power, she can attain up to 12 knots with her 1,400 horsepower Diesel. She has a range of 8,000 miles under power at her cruising speed of eight knots.

Unlike many sail-training vessels, *Esmeralda* is armed. She carries four 5.7 centimeter guns. The ship was named for a Chilean warship credited with sea victories in the 1879 Nitrate War against Bolivia and Peru.

Malcolm Mackenzie

GLORIA
COLUMBIA

This lovely bark could well be called Colombia's gem of the ocean. She was built of steel in Bilbao, Spain, in 1968. *Gloria* is somewhat similar to *Eagle*, although 40 feet shorter, with her overall length of 255 feet. Her beam measures 35 feet and she carries 150 persons, including 15 officers, 45 crew members and 90 trainees of the Colombian Navy. She is equipped to carry provisions for remaining at sea as long as 60 days.

A winged figurehead graces the bow of the *Gloria*. With her 500 horsepower Diesel engine she is able to make 10.5 knots. Her sail area is about 15,000 square feet and her mast height is 130 feet.

One of this bark's distinguishing features is a raised bridge and enclosed pilothouse forward of the mizzenmast.

Norman J. Brouwer

DANMARK
DENMARK

No nation has a longer record in sail-training than Denmark; that country has used sail-training for at least 300 years. Today, the Danish government gives training under sail to boys, 15 to 20 years old, ambitious for careers as officers in the Danish Merchant Marine. The young men are sent for cruises on *Danmark*, a 252-foot full-rigged ship, which carries 80 trainees.

The cruises normally take six months and usually go around the world. The ship and its crew are famous for the salute they give in port, by "manning the yards." The white-uniformed crew stands on the yards, high above the deck, hands stretched out to each other.

At sea, the trainees are given intensive education in mathematics, physics, mechanical engineering and hygiene, as well as navigation, radio technique, winds and currents, meteorology and ship construction. In addition, they get the usual sail-training, performing tasks aboard ship from washing dishes to assisting the surgeon. The ship makes a point of entering and leaving ports under sail if possible.

Danmark was launched in 1932. In 1940, she happened to be in Florida when the German Army occupied Denmark. After Pearl Harbor, the ship was offered to the U.S. government, and was used as a Coast Guard training vessel, with the Danish officers in charge of instruction. In 1945, the vessel returned to her own country; in 1959, the ship was renovated and modernized.

Danmark was designed by Aage Larsen. Her hull is steel. She has a beam of 33 feet and a draft of 17 feet. The vessel carries 26 sails with a total area of 17,600 square feet and her rig is 130 feet high. With her 486 horsepower Diesel, she makes 9.5 knots in calm seas. The ship has a double bottom.

Norman J. Brouwer

GUAYAS
ECUADOR

Guayas, built in Spain in 1977 for Ecuador, is a bark very similar to Colombia's ship, *Gloria*, built in Spain a year later. Both are among the newer sail-training vessels. *Guayas*, who gets her name from the first steamship built in South America, has sailed around the world.

The 914-ton ship accommodates 180 persons. In addition to student midshipmen, she sometimes takes along honor cadets from other service academies of Ecuador.

The beam of this training ship measures 35 feet and her draft is 14 feet; she is powered by a 700 horsepower Diesel engine. Her sparred length is 268 feet; the height of her rig is 127 feet.

SIR WINSTON CHURCHILL
ENGLAND

A three-masted schooner, *Sir Winston Churchill* is a 150 foot long British sail-training vessel built in Yorkshire and launched in 1965. The ship has a beam of 27 feet, a draft of 16, and she displaces 299 tons. Sails on two of her masts are gaff-rigged, but the one on the mizzen is Marconi-rigged. She carries two square sails on her foremast; all her masts are aluminum. Her mainmast is 100 feet high. Total sail area is 8,790 feet. The training ship has a 240 horsepower auxiliary engine.

    Sir Winston is operated by a crew of eight officers and three seamen and accommodates 44 cadets, 16 to 21 years of age, who are given sail-training in the British maritime tradition.

Norman J. Brouwer

BELEM
FRANCE

Belem, a 572-ton bark built in 1896, is the last survivor of France's fleet of commercial sailing vessels. She has been rescued, repatriated and restored through a great public and private effort in France after a career that ranged from lowly work hauling coal and live mules to aristocratic service as a private yacht.

Belem was built at Nantes and was first put to work transporting cocoa beans and other goods between Brazil and France. In 1914, she made a quantum leap up the social ladder when the Duke of Westminster bought her and transformed her into a sumptuous yacht accommodating 40 persons. He installed her first engines and generator, painted gun ports on her topsides to give her the appearance of an oldtime corvette, and introduced yachty-looking teak in a handrail for the dining saloon. In 1921, *Belem* was bought by another well-heeled yachtsman, A.E. Guinness, the Irish brewer, who renamed her *Fantome II*. She sailed around the world in 18 months. Next the ship passed to Italian ownership. Her name was changed to *Giorgia Cini* and her rig was changed to barkentine by the substitution of fore-and-aft sails for the square sails on her mainmast. She became a school ship for young sailors in the Adriatic from 1952 to 1976. Toward the end of that period she was sent to a shipyard in Venice for repairs.

Meanwhile interest was developing in France to regain possession of the historic ship. The National Union of Savings Banks of France came to the rescue. In 1979 a deal was made to buy the ship and tow her back to France. The following year a foundation was created to restore and preserve her. The bark rig and the original name were restored and extensive rehabilitation was planned.

Belem made a triumphant return to Paris, where she was outfitted as a museum ship. Tied up at a quay along the left bank of the Seine near the Eiffel Tower, the venerable ship and the tower joined in attracting tourists. Admission fees helped defray the cost of the extensive work needed to return *Belem* fully to sailing condition.

The ship is 180 feet in sparred length, 26.8 feet wide and has a draft of 15 feet. She is privately owned by the Fondation Belem in Paris.

Norman J. Brouwer

PALINURO
ITALY

The 227-foot barkentine, *Palinuro,* now in the Italian Navy, was formerly the *Commandant Louis Richard,* owned by France. She was built in that country, at Nantes, in 1934. Italy purchased her in 1950, renovated and renamed her.

She carries four square sails on her foremast, which is one foot taller than the mainmast. The main and mizzenmasts are gaff-rigged, with topsails. Three staysails are flown between the main and foremasts. *Palinuro* sails at speeds up to 10 knots.

The ship has a beam of 33 feet, draws 16 feet, and her rig is 115 feet high. She displaces 1,341 tons. The sail area is 9,662 feet. Her auxiliary engine is of 375 horsepower. *Palinuro* is used for specialized sail-training, including the training of harbormasters. She carries five officers, 26 seamen and 54 cadets.

Donald Callendar

AMERIGO VESPUCCI
ITALY

One of the largest of the full-rigged ships used by the navies of the world for sail-training, the 330-foot *Amerigo Vespucci* was named for the Italian navigator and explorer who lived from 1451 to 1512, and for whom America was named. The ship was built of steel in 1930, in Italy. Her beam is 50 feet, 10 inches. She carries 7 officers, a crew of 30 and 100 trainees. Her rig is 160 feet high.

Amerigo Vespucci has sailed across the Atlantic many times. One short but notable passage was in 1960, when she carried the Olympic flame from Athens to Italy. About 20 years later, she made an educational tour to countries bordering the Mediterranean, promoting control of pollution of the sea.

This ship is recognized easily not only because of her monumental size, but because she resembles a 19th Century frigate. She has rather high topsides with two bands of white at the levels of her ports on an otherwise black hull.

SØRLANDET
NORWAY

The 216-foot full-rigged ship Sørlandet is named for the southern coastal area of Norway, where she was built at the port of Kristiansand in 1927. She has been a sail-training vessel for most of her long and useful life, except during World War II.

In that period, she became an overcrowded floating prison for deserters from the German army. Some of the prisoners scuttled the ship, probably by opening sea cocks, and she sank in her harbor in northern Norway. After the war, the ship was retrieved from the frigid fiord, was renovated and returned to the mission of giving sail-training to future merchant seamen in 1948.

Years later, she was presented as a gift to the city of Kristiansand. She was repaired again, put into excellent condition to resume carrying trainees in 1980. That year, about 300 youngsters from 10 nations took part in international friendship cruises aboard *Sørlandet*. In 1981, the ship crossed the Atlantic four times.

Like another Norwegian sail training vessel, *Christian Radich*, *Sørlandet* has been a film star. She was in the BBC film, "All I Ask Is a Tall Ship." In addition, she has appeared in television commercials.

Sørlandet is currently owned by a foundation whose board chairman is the mayor of Kristiansand. The governments of Norway and the city pay for routine maintenance of the ship, but she relies on donations, charters and other private sources for operating income. Her owner is the Full-rigged Ship Sørlandet Non-Profit Foundation.

The 559-ton vessel's hull, masts and yards are steel. Her decks are planked with pine. She carries five levels of square sails on each of her three masts—main, lower and upper topsails, gallant and royal. In addition to those 15 square sails, there are 13 fore-and-aft sails: five jibs, a spanker and storm spanker, three mizzen staysails and three main staysails. Most of the sails are of polyester fabric, and their area is 10,360 square feet.

Sørlandet accommodates 70 trainees and 19 crew members. She has tanks for 40 tons of fresh water and has a desalination plant capable of producing three tons of fresh water a day. A 564-horsepower Diesel powers the ship; electricity is produced by a six-cylinder generator. She makes eight knots under power.

The ship carries 400 tons of stone ballast. Her beam is 29.1 feet and her draft is 14.5 feet. Her overall length, excluding the 20-foot bowsprit, is 186 feet. The mainmast is 115 feet above the waterline.

Norman J. Brouwer

Norman J. Brouwer

CHRISTIAN RADICH
NORWAY

Any of the big school ships would make stunning appearances in a movie, but none better than the Norwegian *Christian Radich* which appeared in the film "Windjammer" in 1958.

The 205-foot *Radich* is one of the few ships with male names and there is good reason for it. The estate of Captain Christian Radich, who had been a wealthy merchant and ship owner, contributed to the commissioning of the *Radich* in 1937. The 575-ton, full-rigged ship has a steel hull. Her beam is 33 feet and her draft 15 feet. Her sails have a total area of 14,525 square feet and her rig is 128 feet high. The ship is equipped with a 600 horsepower Diesel engine that will move her at eight knots.

Radich is either a particularly fast ship among square riggers on the seas today, or is sailed with extraordinary skill, for she has won more than her share of sail-training races since 1956, when she won the Dartmouth to Lisbon race in Europe. This ship has crossed the Atlantic many times and has gone up the St. Lawrence Seaway and through the Great Lakes to Chicago, where she was a sensational attraction. It was estimated that more than 35,000 people visited *Radich* there in three days.

As many as 90 boys, 15 to 19 years of age, are given training at one time aboard *Radich.* For three months, they receive both theoretical and practical instruction in all aspects of life aboard a sailing vessel, starting with washing their own clothing and cleaning all parts of the ship. There is emphasis on safety, with instruction in fire protection, handling life boats, swimming and life-saving. When the ship is cruising, the trainees are assigned to sea duty.

As the first stage in the training of young would-be Norwegian seamen, that three months aboard the *Radich* is necessarily a strongly disciplined, rigidly structured, collective regimen. By the time the students go ashore at the end of this introductory training cruise, they will know whether a seaman's life is for them. If a young man is still enthusiastic about a career at sea after the rigors of shipboard living he receives double credit for his initial training aboard the *Radich.* If a trainee decides that the sea life is not for him, he has still benefited from an experience he will remember the rest of his life.

Norman J. Brouwer

SAGRES II
PORTUGAL

This bark from Portugal is a dazzling sight, as is her elder sister-ship, the United States *Eagle*. Both are 295 feet long. *Sagres II* has an unforgettable appearance, because she wears the Maltese Cross on her square sails, and sports a bust of Prince Henry the Navigator for her figurehead. Her tallest mast is 142 feet aloft.

Sagres II was built in 1938 in Germany and, with *Eagle*, became the property of the United States at the end of the World War II. Brazil became her owner in 1948 and Portugal bought her in 1962 to replace *Sagres I*.

The current *Sagres* normally carries 243 persons aboard: 10 officers, a crew of 153 and 80 cadets. Her speed under power is nine knots, and she has a 40 foot beam.

The ship's name comes from the promontory near Cape St. Vincent in southwestern Portugal, from which many explorers departed in the 15th Century. Prince Henry, who was more of a sponsor than a navigator himself, died there in 1460. Shipwatchers admiring the figurehead should honor Prince Henry as one of the earliest backers of oceanic exploration, (from Portugal to the west coast of Africa).

The spanker–the fore-and-aft sail on the bark's third and smallest mast–is in three sections, divided by two gaffs. Many spankers are in two parts, separated by a single gaff.

Sagres II has a sail area of about 20,000 square feet. She carries 52 tons of oil for her two Diesel engines of 750 horsepower each, which give her a top speed of 9.4 knots and a range of 5,450 miles at her cruising speed of 7.5 knots. Earlier in her career, this ship was named *Guanabara* when owned by Brazil, and *Albert Leo Schlageter* when owned by Germany.

Norman J. Brouwer

JUAN SEBASTIAN DE ELCANO
SPAIN

Here is a huge sailing vessel—one of the world's largest—rigged as a topsail schooner. She is a marvelous sight to behold, resembling an out-sized version of recreational yachts, 352 feet long.

Far from being an overgrown wind and water-borne plaything, Spain's *Juan Sebastian De Elcano* is an impressive sail-training ship and one of the few four-masted sailing ships afloat. Her draft is 22.7 feet and her beam is 44 feet. (In spite of the masculine name, this ship, like all others, requires the feminine gender.) She carries 407 persons: 24 officers, a crew of 173 and 210 trainees.

Juan Sebastian is unmistakably an ocean sailer. At 164 feet, her mainmast is too high for many large bridges.

She is a sister ship to Chile's *Esmeralda.* The two have the same hulls but different rigging. While the Spanish ship is a topsail schooner, the Chilean version is a four-masted barkentine. The Spanish ship carries two saluting guns.

Juan Sebastian was named for the first circumnavigator of the world—the man who, after the death of Magellan, succeeded to the command of the 1519-1523 expedition.

Philadelphia Ship Presentation Guild

GAZELA OF PHILADELPHIA
U.S.A.

The barkentine *Gazela* is remarkable because she is the oldest and largest wooden square rigger still able to sail. Her sparred length is 177 feet, 10 inches. She was formerly the Portuguese fishing vessel *Gazela Primeiro* and in that role she sailed every Spring from Lisbon to the Grand Banks to launch her 30 dories from which her men fished for cod. She was built of pine in Portugal in 1883. According to Portuguese legend, the pine was planted in 1460 by Prince Henry the Navigator, specifically for shipbuilding. *Gazela* was first rigged as a topsail schooner and may have served as a whaler before 1900, when she was converted to a barkentine to become a fishing ship.

Originally, the ship relied on sail power alone. She was modernized in 1938 with the addition of a Diesel auxiliary engine along with two generators and an engine to power her anchor windlass. However, the old hand-operated windlass is still in its place.

Visitors going below on the ship can see the extremely crowded conditions in which the fishermen slept, two to a bunk, in three tiers of bunks in the narrow forecastle.

Gazela has a draft of 16 feet, eight inches and carries 8,910 square feet of sail; her beam measures 27 feet, and her mast height is 93 feet, four inches. She is owned by the Philadelphia Ship Preservation Guild and she can be seen at Penn's Landing, on the Delaware River, near the foot of Spruce Street.

The guild's volunteers help to maintain and sail the ship. Among its other activities, the guild is restoring *Nellie and Mary,* a wooden schooner built in 1891, formerly a Delaware Bay oyster dredger and freight hauler.

SEA CLOUD
WEST GERMANY

The largest and most luxurious privately-owned square-rigger in the world is *Sea Cloud,* a four-masted bark. With a sparred length of 316 feet, she is longer than the U.S. Coast Guard's *Eagle.*

Sea Cloud was built in 1931 in Germany as an elegant yacht for Marjorie Merriweather Post, heiress to a cereal fortune, and her husband, Edward F. Hutton. The steel-hulled vessel cost $1.2 million in 1931 dollars. During World War II, the U.S. Navy leased the ship for convoy duty.

After the war, Mrs. Post retained her palatial yacht for four years, and she is reported to have spent $3 million in refitting and operating costs.

Sea Cloud's next owner was General Rafael Trujillo, dictator of the Dominican Republic, who renamed the ship *Patria.* A later owner changed her name to *Atarna* and used the ship as a floating university.

The name has reverted to the original *Sea Cloud.* She was again refurbished in 1978, and partially rebuilt inside to have more staterooms, which currently number 41. Now, she is an opulent cruise ship plying the Caribbean and Mediterranean with private parties.

Sea Cloud's dimensions are impressive: The ship displaces 2,323 tons. She is 49 feet wide and has a draft of 16.5 feet. She has four 9-cylinder Diesel engines driving two propellers. Those engines have an output of 6,000 horsepower and can move the ship at 15 knots. Her range is 10,000 miles and her crew numbers 60.

The 49-foot beam allows ample room for a sumptuous main saloon with deck to ceiling bookcases and a grand piano. The dining saloon is also capacious. The ship has her own small "hospital" on one of the three decks.

The ship's sail plan shows four jibs and staysails at the bowsprit and bow, three masts with five square sails each and the jigger mast at the stern with a spanker. Above the spanker is a topsail called in this case a jigger upper staysail. In addition, when the wind is right, the ship can spread six staysails between the masts. There is no doubt that *Sea Cloud* can spread a glorious cloud of canvas.

EAGLE
U.S.A.

The beautiful bark, *Eagle,* is the sail-training vessel of the U.S. Coast Guard, carrying 180 trainees in addition to 19 officers and a crew of 46, for a total of 245 persons on board. She was built in Germany for sail-training in 1936 and was acquired by the United States as part of Germany's war reparations after having served as a cargo ship in World War II. The 295-foot ship is virtually unchanged under American ownership, except that the fore-and-aft sail on the mizzenmast is a single gaff spanker instead of a double. Her hull is steel; her rig is 148 feet high and her beam is 39 feet; her draft is 17 feet. *Eagle* displaces 1,784 tons.

Trainees handling *Eagle* must learn to deal with more than 25,300 square feet of

Norman J. Brouwer

sails and more than 20 miles of rigging, as well as her 700 horsepower Diesel engine. Cadets in the lower classes of the Coast Guard Academy learn to serve as the ship's crew, while the upper classmen and women serve as her officers.

There are three sister ships of *Eagle* owned by other nations: *Mircea* of Romania, *Sagres II* of Portugal and *Tovarisch II* of the Soviet Union.

Eagle goes on one to five-week cruises from her base at New London, Connecticut, during the warm months. She can sail up to 18 knots under favorable wind conditions. Under power, she can make 10.5 knots and has a range of 5,450 miles cruising at 7.5 knots.

Norman J. Brouwer

KRUZENSTERN
SOVIET UNION

The largest of all the sail-training vessels, larger even than *Esmeralda* and her sister ship, *Juan Sebastian de Elcano,* is another four-masted vessel, the Soviet Union's 378-foot bark, *Kruzenstern.* Unlike most other national sail-training ships, she is attached to the Ministry of Fisheries, rather than to the Navy or the Coast Guard.

This mammoth ship accommodates 236 persons, including 26 officers, 50 crew members and 160 trainees. Her beam is a broad 46 feet, her draft is 25 feet, and her sail area is more than 36,000 voluminous square feet. Her mainmast is 162 feet high.

This vessel was named for Ivan F. Kruzenstern who, in 1803 to 1806, led the first Russian round-the-world scientific expedition, and subsequently published several works based on that long voyage.

Kruzenstern is distinguished not only by her heroic size, but by her lifeboats, which are carried high above the deck in davits. She has a double spanker and topsail on her fourth mast.

The ship, built in 1926, hauled nitrate from Chile, and grain from Australia, before she was taken over by the Soviet Union, in 1946. Previously, she had been named *Padua.*

Norman J. Brouwer

TOVARISCH
SOVIET UNION

The Soviet Union's bark, *Tovarisch,* is one of four similar but not identical ships built in Hamburg, Germany. The others are *Eagle, Mircea,* and *Sagres II. Tovarisch* was built in 1933 and was originally the *Gorch Fock* of the German Navy, which has another ship by that name now.

Tovarisch has a beam of 39 feet, four inches and her draft is 17 feet. She carries 18,400 square feet of sails. Her mainmast is 135 feet and her sparred length is 270 feet.

The vessel sank in 1945 and was refloated by Soviet salvage workers three years later. In 1951, she joined the Soviet Navy as a sail-training vessel. (The Soviet Union had a previous ship by the same name—a four-masted bark that had once been called *Lauriston.*)

There are several acceptable ways of spelling *Tovarisch,* which is, of course, an English rendition of the Russian. Some prefer to spell it "Tovaristsch". However it's spelled, the word means comrade.

Norman J. Brouwer

ALEXANDRIA
UNITED STATES

The three-masted topsail schooner *Alexandria* is a familiar sight at gatherings of Tall Ships and waterfront celebrations, distinguished by her red sails, including two square sails at the top of her foremast. She was widely known under her former name of Lindø, which was changed in 1983 when she was acquired by the Alexandria Seaport Foundation.

The ship has had a varied history, with different rigs, different missions and different engines since she was launched in 1929 in Sweden as *Yngve,* and put to work as a bulk cargo carrier in the Baltic and North Seas. After 10 years of service, which included fishing for herring north of Iceland, she was sold and renamed *Lindö,* a Swedish term standing for "island of Linden trees." In 1957 she was re-rigged as a two-masted vessel, and 10 years later she was altered again to become a motor ship.

Major changes were made in 1975 when the ship was rebuilt in Denmark, converted for passenger carrying and re-rigged as a topsail schooner. The Danish punctuation of the name was used, making it *Lindø.* An 185-horsepower Diesel was installed, replacing a 150 horsepower engine which had followed the original 90 horsepower plant. The vessel then was used in the charter trade in the Caribbean and began taking part in Tall Ships races. In 1976 she placed third in her class in the race from England to New York. She took second place in her class in 1980 in a race from Boston to Norway. In 1982 she appeared in the film "The Island," and the following year she arrived in Alexandria and was re-named for the city. There she promotes interest in the city's historic seaport and in the foundation's education programs in celestial navigation and wooden boat building. In addition, teenagers get apprentice sail training on the ship.

Alexandria has an overall length of 125 feet. The vessel displaces 176 tons, and has a beam of 22 feet and a draft of 10. Heavily constructed, her planking is three-inch oak and her frames are eight-inch oak. Her 11 sails offer more than 7,000 square feet of area to the wind. The ship is luxurious below decks, where she has a spacious salon and five double staterooms.

Norman J. Brouwer

HARVEY GAMAGE
UNITED STATES

In 1973, the Harvey Gamage shipyard in South Bristol, Maine, built this 115-foot schooner, named for the master shipbuilder. He has many other wooden vessels to his credit, including *Clearwater,* the Hudson River crusading sloop, and *Shenandoah,* a topsail schooner that sails out of Martha's Vineyard in the summer months.

   Harvey Gamage has a beam of 23 feet, seven inches, a draft of nine feet, seven inches and displaces 129 tons. Her sail area is 4,200 square feet. The schooner has a Diesel engine of 120 horsepower. Her rig is 91 feet high. She sails out of Charlotte Amalie in the Virgin Islands in the winter and out of Rockland, Maine, in the summer, carrying passengers on cruises or groups of young people for sail-training.

Sail Training

Ship-watchers can thank the idea of "sail-training" for the abundance of large Tall Ships afloat today. These beautiful vessels, the last great square-riggers and some of the largest schooners on the sea, exist because the many nations that own them believe fervently in the value of "on deck" training for young people preparing for careers on ships in the merchant marine or the armed forces. Most of the sailing ships we admire so intensely are owned by navy and coast guard forces, including *Eagle*, training ship of the U.S. Coast Guard.

Clearly all the young men and women trained on these ships do not plan careers aboard square-riggers. Many leaders of navies and merchant marine services are convinced that serving at sea, under fair weather and foul, is vital training. A ship's officer must first be a fully competent seaman, they believe, and aboard a sailing vessel can learn to be a better sailor and a better shipmate.

Behind that belief is the realization that a sailing ship must be operated in harmony with the wind and the sea, both often unpredictable and sometimes life-threatening. So, learning good seamanship is necessary for survival, and an important ingredient in this learning is the ability to work in harmony with one's shipmates.

For the young participants, the sail-training process becomes an unparalleled push for maturity through the challenge of sharing life in a constricted space and facing the dangers of the sea, where there is no place to run and no place to hide. Trainees recognize swiftly the absolute need to accept direction and instruction, learning to accept the need for discipline among the crew. They realize that each crew member is dependent on the others—all at risk on the sea together often in a situation where unity is required for strength. Understanding the importance of the individual's contribution to the successful operation of the ship, trainees derive satisfaction and pride in their ability to work well for the good of the group, rising to the demands of the situation created by an environment they cannot escape or control.

The concept of sail-training, long embraced successfully as part of career education by governments, has been adapted widely by private agencies not otherwise connected with the sea. Their aim is to extract similar benefits from shorter term sail-training for young boys and girls, usually from 15 to 19 years old. Many of these have heard of the advantages of shipboard experience. Some are looking for adventure; others are attracted to the sea or simply know they like sailing. Still others are special groups, such as troubled youngsters, who are sent to sea on sail-training ships to learn self-discipline and responsibility in innovative programs.

In other cases, sail-training has been combined with education in subjects related to the sea, such as oceanography. That educational experience is offered at both high school and college levels.

Sail-training has also been rewarding when used with physically handicapped persons. The Jubilee Sailing Trust of England encourages able-bodied and handicapped individuals to work side by side on its training vessel. The able-bodied learn from the disabled that one can cope despite handicaps. They all learn to get things done regardless of the obstacles—an essential ingredient of seamanship. In the U.S., on the north shore of Long Island, volunteers are restoring the bugeye *Little Jennie*, with the idea of sailing her with handicapped persons in the crew.

The privately owned vessels in sail-training for young people include many of the most handsome Tall Ships, other than the big square-riggers. Many are large schooners.

An example is *Rambler*, a three-masted staysail schooner, 106 feet long, operated by the Ocean Research and Education Society of Gloucester, Mass., which has a "sail and study" program for college students. It offers an alternate semester of work in the marine sciences for which students receive college credit. Students spend six weeks at the society's classroom and laboratory facility at Gloucester, and six weeks aboard *Rambler*. The vessel takes up to 20 students, who study such subjects as the ecology of coral reefs and the habitat and behavior of humpback whales.

The 130-foot schooner, *Western Union*, is used by VisionQuest, a private agency, in one of its treatment undertakings for youngsters referred from the criminal justice or mental health systems. The organizations states: "The basic tenets of sail-training —development of a sense of responsibility, rigorous self-discipline, and respect for authority—are the basic treatment aims for a majority of troubled youth." In life aboard ship, the trainees "learn to prepare for adversity and emergency. They learn to function effectively in the most stressful situations, in the wake of great emotion. The youths who have completed the sailing program display a self-confidence and assurance which is evident in those who have successfully met the challenge of the sea."

Western Union goes on voyages. Some of the sail-training vessels go out for weekends or other short periods, and do not venture far from land; others go on longer cruises.

Among the sail-training vessels on the West Coast is *Adventuress*, a 101-foot wooden schooner operated by Youth Adventure, Inc., of Mercer Island, Washington. She carries groups of 25 to 30 trainees who go on weekend sails in autumn, winter and spring, and on longer trips during the summer. Many of the participants are Sea Explores and Girl Scouts.

A 156-foot schooner has been the home of a sail training program for learning disabled students. The student crew of 28 comes from high schools and junior high schools. They receive instruction in marine studies, while experiencing the discipline and cooperation essential for life at sea.

Tabor Academy of Marion, Mass., operates *Tabor Boy*, a 92-foot schooner, on which boys 14 to 17 years old go on three-week summer cruises for sail-training, and for longer cruises in spring and autumn, when studies in oceanography are added to the training.

Sail-training is offered to young persons in Canada, as well as in the United States. Toronto Brigantines, Inc., of Toronto, Ontario, owns *Pathfinder* and *Playfair*, both brigantines operating during the warm months on the Great Lakes and the St. Lawrence River.

The broad attraction of sailing on Tall Ships can also be used to educate the public about the the environment while on short cruises. The Hudson River sloop *Clearwater* is a crusader in that specialized education.

From these examples, it is plain that there are many aspects of sail-training, with learning how to sail as an elementary first part. All of the programs strive to go far beyond training in sailing, to utilize the emotional impact of the sea on human beings, to mold character and to educate.

Sail Training Races

Many of the gatherings of Tall Ships are arranged to celebrate special events, such as the centennial of the Statue of Liberty in New York Harbor in 1986, but many others occur because of races in which the large sail-training vessels compete. Often, schedules are arranged so that the races end at places where a special event is being celebrated, and a parade of Tall Ships becomes a spectacular feature.

It seems perfectly natural that the large square-riggers of the world would race against each other so that their crews could sharpen their skills and enjoy the competition. Actually, they have been doing so only since 1956. The idea for international sail-training ship races was conceived by a London barrister named Bernard Morgan. He talked to many people about his idea of a brotherhood of the sea, fostered by friendly rivalry among the young sailors on training ships.

His crusading drew some enthusiastic followers, and in 1954, Captain John Illingworth, a famous ocean racing skipper, formed the Sail Training International Race Committee. This was the group that organized the first Tall Ships race from Torbay, England to Lisbon, Portugal, and developed a system of handicapping that resulted in the birth of the Sail Training Association in 1956. Illingworth was its first chairman and Bernard Morgan its secretary. The race they sponsored in 1968 drew 17 entries. Since that time the Association has continued to schedule races and cruises for sail-training ships, square-riggers, schooners and others, and to spread the gospel of sail-training.

In 1972, an American citizen, Barclay Warburton, sailed his brigantine *Black Pearl* to Europe to take part in the Tall Ships races. He was inspired to start an American organization similar in aims to those of the Sail Training Association. In 1973, the American Sail Training Association was formed as an affiliate of the British association. It has offices at Newport, R.I.

ASTA strives to get young people to the sea in deepwater sailing ships. The reasons, ASTA says are:
Sail training is an adventure and an educational and character-building experience for young people. International good will results when the sail training ships from around the world are gathered in a spirit of camaraderie and friendly competition. These activities result in greater awareness of, and appreciation for the values of our shared maritime tradition.

"ASTA organizes sail-training races in the Atlantic and the Pacific, and promotes sail-training on great square-riggers and scores of other ships where experienced sailors offer a combination of adventure and training to young trainees. Membership in ASTA is open to all interested persons. When the Tall Ships assemble for special events in the U.S., whether planned by ASTA or not, that organization cooperates in arrangements to welcome the trainees and provide activities for them."

The tradition of holding sail-training races every two years continues. The Tall Ships races are usually held in even-numbered years, but local races may be added in odd-numbered years.

Races are often scheduled and routes prepared to bring the Tall Ships to a special festival at a port city. This occurred in 1984, when the ships congregated in Quebec in honor of the 450th anniversary of Jacques Cartier's discovery of the St. Lawrence River. And now, incidentally, there is a Canadian Sail Training Association.

At times the squares-riggers and other Tall Ships assemble at the request of others, particularly the various Operation Sail groups which have functioned temporarily to plan and advertise specific envents. Operation Sail '76 brought the Tall Ships to New York harbor to celebrate the 200th birthday of the United States, and Tall Ships '82 drew them to Philadelphia to commemorate the 300th anniversary of William Penn's arrival aboard the ship *Welcome*.

History Comes Alive!

Famous Replicas

Many replicas or near-replicas of revered ships of the past have been built in recent decades as appreciation and understanding of American seafaring history has increased. In this section, we report on some of the more interesting replicas that Tall Ship enthusiasts will enjoy seeing.

No attempt is made to distinguish between true replicas—exact in all details—and the near-replicas which look like the originals, but may have been modified in many hidden but important features of construction. A replica built to sit quietly outside a museum and never go to sea could be built to be an exact duplicate of the original. However, replicas intended to sail on the ocean with passengers must meet modern standards of safety at sea that the originals could not meet today. One can therefore expect watertight bulkheads and whatever modification it takes to insure stability in replicas intended to sail with passengers. These and other safety features were never in the original ships.

Skillfully crafted replicas, built by oldtime methods, look like the originals, and are a delight to behold, and in some cases, to board for a taste of sailing as it was long ago. When one sails on *Sea Lion*, for example, the pleasure and excitement at stepping on a 16th Century square-rigged vessel that actually takes passengers is undiminished by the knowledge that the ship may sail legally with passengers on inland waters but would not meet current standards for an ocean voyage.

Some replicas are built to sail with their crews, but not to carry passengers. Examples are *Dove* and *Pride of Baltimore*. Others are built mainly to be part of a re-creation of an old waterfront scene. An example is *Globe*.

In all cases, replicas are living history. They bring to life a significant part of the history of the nation and the world that no words, paintings, photographs, film or television re-enactments can equal. They show us in their unique way: this is how it was.

Stanley Witkowski, Jr., Dupont Co.

PRIDE OF BALTIMORE
UNITED STATES

The graceful topsail schooner, *Pride of Baltimore,* is a replica of the famous, speedy Baltimore clippers of the early 19th Century, but not a reproduction of any particular clipper. The clippers, like other ships of that period and earlier, were built from models, rather than from drawings, and no models survive. She was designed by Thomas Gillmer, and was commissioned in 1977.

The name may truthfully reflect the city's pride in its ship, but it also has another meaning. *Pride of Baltimore* was the affectionate name of an earlier clipper, the *Chasseur,* captained by Thomas Boyle, one of the most successful privateers active in the War of 1812. The ship's achievements were due not only to her speed but to her maneuverability under the skilled direction of Boyle.

Pride of Baltimore is a 121-ton vessel, with an overall length of 136 feet, a beam of 22 feet eight inches, and a draft of nine feet nine inches. Her mainmast is 92 feet high. She is powered by an 85 horsepower Diesel. She is distinctive among schooners because of her sharply raking masts.

Her futtocks (frame sections) were put together with foot-long locust trunnels (tree nails), left "standing proud", that is, not sawed flush with the frames, in accordance with Chesapeake Bay boatbuilding practice of the last century.

Pride of Baltimore was built of better woods than her 19th Century ancestors, many of which were constructed of unseasoned lumber. Machich and bullettree were used for *Pride's* keel; her frames are mostly of Santa Maria, and her stem, sternpost and keelson were carved from bullettree. All are tropical hardwoods. Longleaf yellow pine, two and one-quarter inches thick, was the planking for the hull and deck. The spars were fashioned from Douglas fir. Rosewood was chosen for the tiller and the belaying pins.

A variety of sails on the *Pride of Baltimore* add up to an area of 7,000 square feet. The mainsail, foresail and staysail are made of heavy cotton duck. The jib and square fore-topsail are woven of flax, while the other sails are fashioned from lighter cotton. *Pride of Baltimore* was not designed to carry passengers as she has only five feet of headroom. The ship has made long voyages in her primary mission as goodwill ambassador of the city whose name she bears.

CLEARWATER
UNITED STATES

Clearwater is a replica of the type of sloop that used to be common on the Hudson River about 150 years ago, before the advent of the steamboat, tug-hauled barges, and the railroads. Building the replica was suggested by Pete Seeger, the folksinger and outspoken environmentalist.

An organization of river lovers was created to build the graceful sloop and send her out to carry a message of care and concern for the Hudson's health. *Clearwater* is the flagship of their crusade. Cyrus Hamlin designed the replica and she was built at the Harvey Gamage boatyard in South Bristol, Maine, in 1968.

This gaff-rigged wooden sloop was launched in 1969. She has an overall length of 106 feet, including a bowsprit. Her beam is 25 feet and her mast towers 108 feet. Her owner is Hudson River Sloop Clearwater, Inc., of Poughkeepsie, an environmental organization striving to promote the clean-up of the Hudson, the improvement of its water quality and restoration of the waterfront.

The group conducts three and five-hour educational sails aboard *Clearwater,* with instruction in history, biology and environmental science for children and adults. Their gospel reaches not only the 12,000 annually who get to cruise on *Clearwater,* but the hundreds and thousands who see the sloop sailing up and down the Hudson, or at the many festive celebrations during the year at riverside towns in which *Clearwater* and her crusade star.

CALIFORNIAN
UNITED STATES

Californian is one of three large, lovely schooners built since 1976 with the guidance of Melbourne Smith, either as builder, in the case of *Pride of Baltimore,* or designer, as with *Spirit of Massachusetts,* or both, as with *Californian.*

She is based on the lines of an 1849 Revenue Marine cutter. *Californian* is a faithful re-creation on the outside. Inside, she meets modern requirements for carrying passengers and also has some touches of elegance, including a governor's cabin panelled in rosewood, and two luxuriously appointed staterooms. The ship boasts furnishings that include antique chairs, sofas and desk.

Californian has a clipper bow with a long jib boom and a figurehead of Queen Calafia, carved by Frank James Morgan. Calafia is a mythical Amazon queen who appears in a 16th century Spanish romance novel as the ruler of an island in the Pacific called California. Like *Pride of Baltimore,* this schooner sets two square sails on her foremast. Also like *Pride,* the lumber for her backbone is a very dense wood from Central America. However, in *Californian,* the frames are laminated, like the roof beams in some modern churches. She wears an iron ballast keel, cast in Pennsylvania. On her transom, she sports an unusual amount of colorful ornamentation, carved in low relief. At the center is a large spread eagle of the type that government revenue cutters displayed. Beside it are the seal of California on the port side and the revenue seal on the starboard. Next to them are two carved bears, facing the eagle. This is probably the most intricately designed transom on any of today's Tall Ships.

As befits a revenue cutter, she carries six bronze cannons. They are six-pounders, used to fire salutes. The ship is used for limited charters, in addition to sail-training, and charter guests are greeted by a roaring salute in addition to the sound of bos'n's pipes, and by the crew dressed in the splendor of period naval uniforms.

The main mission of *Californian* is to provide sail-training to 14 cadets at a time, for 11-day sessions. The vessel sails along the California coast all year 'round, stopping at 15 ports. The concentrated training course covers shipboard safety, standing lookout, marlinspike seamanship, sail and line handling, helmsmanship, meteorology, coastal piloting and use of shipboard equipment. Above and beyond all the proficiency training is the "main course", as on all sail-training ships—self-discipline, responsibility and teamwork. At times, *Californian* makes longer voyages; she has sailed to the Hawaiian Islands. In 1985 *Californian* made a goodwill cruise to Mexico hauling shelter supplies for earthquake victims.

This sail-training ship has a sparred length of 145 feet, a beam of 24 feet three inches and her draft is nine feet five inches. On a rig 98 feet high, she carries 7,400 square feet of sails. She is powered by a 140-horsepower Diesel. The 135-ton ship is owned by the Nautical Heritage Society, Dana Point, Calif.

SPIRIT OF MASSACHUSETTS
UNITED STATES

The 138-ton *Spirit of Massachusetts,* commissioned in 1984, is a 125-foot gaff-rigged fishing schooner with topsails. She was built outdoors at the Charlestown Navy Yard at Boston, Massachusetts, by New England Historic Seaport. The ship was designed by Melbourne Smith, who built both *Pride of Baltimore* and *Californian.* The owners call her *SSS Spirit of Massachusetts,* with the letters standing for "Sailing School Ship." Her triple mission is to serve as a training ship for sea education programs, to prove herself a goodwill ambassador for the Commonwealth of Massachusetts, and to be a charter vessel for day sails, for dockside receptions and special events.

The seaport views *Spirit* as a descendant of the Edward Burgess – designed *Fredonia,* a Gloucester fishing schooner widely imitated in the fishing fleets of New England between 1890 and 1910. She may thus be regarded as a "type replica." Her hull has a V-shaped bottom and rounded topsides.

Much of the wood used in building this ship came from the eastern United States. The white oak for her frames was found in Massachusetts, while most of the longleaf pine for the hull planking and interior surfaces came from the South. Other woods used include locust, white pine, tamarack, red spruce and green heart—a tropical hardwood resistant to rot, used in the keel.

Frames for *Spirit* were assembled from four to 14 futtocks (frame sections), fastened together with trunnels (tree nails or pegs), of black locust from Pennsylvania. She was built using traditional methods and tools of the old days—the adze, and old "spuds" and "slicks", which are large chisels. These were augmented by modern power tools, including chain saws and powered planes and drills. Unlike the fishing schooners she resembles, *Spirit of Massachusetts* has the latterday advantage of outside lead ballast, bolted to her keel.

She has a beam of 24 feet and a draft of 10 feet. The white-hulled schooner's top mast truck is 100.6 feet above the waterline. She can accommodate a crew of 10. She daysails with 50 passengers and can host 75 persons at dockside. Powered by a 130 horsepower Diesel, she carries 585 gallons of fuel. She also has tanks for 600 gallons of water.

Marcus Halevi

SEA LION
UNITED STATES

Seeing a ship replica in his youth gave one man an obsession with the idea of building another–and he did it. Ernest Cowan, like thousands of other tourists, inspected *Mayflower II* at Plymouth, Massachusetts, while on a vacation trip. It struck him that it would be a great accomplishment to build a ship of the same period that would really sail, instead of being permanently attached to her dock. Then, he reasoned, people could be better able to visualize and appreciate what it was like to sail on a small ship as the Pilgrims did.

Cowan did copious research. In 1971, he found information in a treatise published in England in 1586, on the design of the three-masted, square-rigged merchant ship of the Elizabethan period. The *Sea Lion* is name for C.E. Lyon, Cowan's friend, a lumber mill owner, who found virgin white oak for the ship's frames and donated use of his mill to cut the lumber. The oak was also contributed to the project. The keel was laid in 1977. Years of volunteer labor and financial contributions from the public went into the realization of Cowan's dream, and huge obstacles were overcome. It has been estimated that 70,000 man-hours of labor were invested in the construction of this hand-made ship.

Sea Lion was launched in 1984. She is about 40 feet long on deck; her bowsprit extends her overall length to 63 feet. The rig height is 58 feet. Her sails, made of flax from Scotland, have a total area of 1,300 square feet. She is a 90-ton vessel, and is one on which a person can indeed visualize how our earliest immigrants sailed to the New World, but she'll never be subjected to ocean waves. *Sea Lion* sails on Lake Chautauqua, from her home port at Mayville, New York.

Sea Lion was rigged–another major undertaking–using 9,000 pounds of hemp line from Denmark. She was commissioned in the summer of 1985 and tested under sail. She is owned by Sea Lion Project Limited, a membership organization the public is invited to join. The address is: R.D., One Sea Lion Drive, Mayville, N.Y. 14757. *Sea Lion* swings on a mooring firmly chained to a burial vault that contains four tons of concrete.

Stanley Witkowski, Jr., Dupont Co.

BLUENOSE II
CANADA

The 160-foot gaff-rigged schooner, *Bluenose II* is a replica of the famous Grand Banks fishing schooner of the same name, pictured on the Canadian dime.

The original *Bluenose* won many of the International Fishermen's Races in the 1920's and 1930's, competing with boats from New England. The replica was built in 1961 in Lunenburg, Nova Scotia, in the same yard that built the original. She is used for charters and for public cruises. The vessel normally carries three officers and 10 crew members, and her home port is Lunenburg. She carries 12,550 square feet of sails and has a beam of 27 feet. She gracefully combines large size and beauty under sail with her 125-foot rig. To many people the Nova Scotia schooner is the epitome of the classic schooner and *Bluenose II* is the well-loved living example.

Norman J. Brouwer

BILL OF RIGHTS
UNITED STATES

A wooden replica of an 1856 schooner, *Bill of Rights* is 151 feet overall. She was built at the Harvey Gamage yard in South Bristol, Maine, and is gaff-rigged, with topsails. Her home port is Newport, R.I., where she works as a passenger-carrying vessel. The 99.8 ton schooner has 6,300 square feet of sail and her rig height is 115 feet.

Norman J. Brouwer

DOVE
UNITED STATES

After a three-month crossing from England, described as "boysterous", two ships carrying colonists landed near the mouth of the Potomac River in 1634. They were the 100-foot *Ark* and 56-foot *Dove,* with about 140 settlers who founded the colony of Maryland. They landed at a small bay and called their settlement St. Mary's City. It became the early capital of Maryland.

In 1975, the state decided to build a replica of the *Dove.* William Avery Baker designed the ship and Cambridge shipbuilder James B. Richardson, who had been building wooden boats for 50 years, came out of retirement to re-create *Dove.*

The replica was finished in 1978 and sailed across Chesapeake Bay to her home port of St. Mary's City. During the temperate months, Dove sails around the bay, spreading goodwill and illuminating history with the beguiling spectacle of a 350-year old square-rigged ship. She is a colorful attraction at waterfront celebrations, and a solid illustration that enlivens a visitor's curiosity about the nation's history.

Dove has a sparred length of 76 feet and is 56 feet long on deck. The 42-ton vessel has a beam of 17 feet and a draft of six feet. Her mainmast is 59 feet tall and her sails have an area of approximately 1,965 square feet.

The ship is steered by an outboard rudder, directly connected to a long tiller on the high poop deck. Near the bow, a massive oak windlass is available to raise the 300-pound anchor. The mammoth anchor is in place, looking very impressive, but a modern lightweight anchor is used to avoid the back-breaking toil of handling the authentic but weighty replica. A crew of seven sails the ship. She does not carry passengers.

Dove is a pinnace—a 17th Century three-masted square rigger, smaller than the full-rigged ships of that period, and similar to the galleon, such as *Mayflower.* She is square-rigged on her fore-and mainmasts and carries a lateen sail on her mizzen. The square sail forward is a spritsail attached to a spritsail yard which pivots on the bowsprit. On each of the fore and mainmasts are two square sails. The mizzen carries a lateen sail on a dipping yard—a yard that is always "dipped" or carried around to the lee side of the mast when the ship changes tack.

Vessels with a rig of this type do not sail well upwind, which is why they spend time waiting for favorable winds. They sail well with winds on the beam or further aft. However, in trying to sail up wind, *Dove* cannot come about in less than 120 degrees and makes so much leeway that she cannot make progress, as later square-rigged vessels did and as fore-and-aft rigged vessels do so much more efficiently today.

Dove is colorful to see. Her hull is painted red and yellow at the bow and red and blue at the stern. The hull is heavily built of white oak, and her deck is yellow pine from Maryland. Near the tiller is a wooden binnacle with a candle lantern glowing dimly on a primitive gimballed compass.

Down below, among sparse accommodations for her small crew, *Dove* has a bricked square area on which a fire could be made for cooking. An opening above carries off the smoke.

A considerable amount of research has been done to assure the authenticity of the crew's clothing, and the crew provides an impressive re-enactment of the way sailors looked 350 years ago, head-gear included. The sailors are knowledgeable about their ship and are ready to answer all questions, and to explain the workings and equipment of the ship to visitors.

During the winter months, repair and refurbishment goes on at St. Mary's City.

Norman J. Brouwer

ROSE
UNITED STATES

The original *Rose* was a British frigate, built in 1756 in Yorkshire. Her great claim to fame on this side of the Atlantic was her role in the American Revolution. In 1775 and part of the 1776, *Rose* was based at Newport, R.I., as flagship of a squadron sent to prevent smuggling. Colonial Rhode Island's affluent smugglers, who were evading British taxes, responded by convincing farmers not to sell food to the fleet. The British tried to force the farmers to supply them, and the next move was an attempt to fire on the ships with old cannons. The British then closed Narragansett Bay to all shipping. From all that friction came the first proposal to create an American navy in 1775—even before the Declaration of Independence.

Rose convoyed British ships along the American Coast, during the Revolutionary War. In 1779, when a French fleet was reported on its way to help the beleaguered colonists, the British scuttled *Rose* across the channel to the harbor of Savannah, barring the entry of the French.

Various pieces of the original *Rose* have been recovered, and were used in the replica, built in 1969 in Nova Scotia by John Millar, architectural historian of Newport. The replica sailed out of Newport in the 1970's. By 1980, she was suffering from rot in her planking; in 1985, she was being rebuilt at Bridgeport, Conn.

The term "frigate" in the period of the original *Rose* meant a warship with 20 to 40 guns. She actually carried up to 42. Her replica has a sparred length of 170 feet and a beam of 31 feet. She draws about 13 feet and her three-masted rig, 130 feet high, supports 13,000 square feet of Dacron sails. The vessel displaces 500 tons. The replica was constructed from original plans deposited at the National Maritime Museum, Greenwich, England. Her figurehead is a growling lion—or is it a lioness named Rose?

Norman J. Brouwer

MAYFLOWER II
UNITED STATES

One of the oldest and most popular replicas in the United States is *Mayflower II*, docked at Plymouth, Mass. She was built in 1957 and was sailed across the Atlantic in a symbolic voyage from England to Plymouth Rock by Alan Villiers, in the path of the Pilgrims of 1620.

The limits on the sailing ability of ships of this type is demonstrated by the fact that the Pilgrims intended to land in Virginia, but strong winds, not errors in navigation, took them hundreds of miles further north. Villiers however, reported that the high sterncastle on the ship did not present a problem in her sailing.

The *Mayflower II* is a three-masted galleon, 65 feet long and 26 feet wide, displacing 180 tons. Her draft is 11 feet. Her rig is similar to that of *Dove,* a pinnace of the same period. There is a small square sail forward on a sprit. Her foremast and mainmast carry two square sails each, and her mizzenmast supports a lateen sail.

Mayflower II's hull has a round bottom and then curves gently inward above the waterline. She has a long, straight keel and a heavy bowsprit, and several ports for guns. The original was launched from Plymouth, England in 1615.

Mayflower II was designed by William Avery Baker, who also designed *Dove* and produced preliminary plans for *Elizabeth II.*

Norman J. Brouwer

SHENANDOAH
UNITED STATES

Like *Californian*, *Shenandoah* is a replica of a revenue cutter. She is a topsail schooner setting two square sails on her foremast as well as a topsail on her mainmast. Altogether, her sails add up to 7,000 square feet. The schooner has a sparred length of 108 feet, and her rig is 94 feet high. She has a beam of 23 feet and a draft of 11.

Shenandoah was built by the Harvey Gamage yard, in Maine. She sails out of Vineyard Haven, Mass., during the summer months, taking passengers on cruises and is also used for sail-training for youth groups.

Tall Ships and Tales

Clippers and Full-Rigged Ships

The clippers of the 19th Century that engaged in trade with China often raced home to England and America with their cargoes of tea. Perhaps the most famous of these races took place in 1866 among 16 clippers. They all left a port on the Min River within a day of each other. During their voyage across the Pacific, around Cape Horn and across the Atlantic to London, they lost sight of one another. Amazingly, five of them arrived off the Scilly Isles together and three of those miraculously docked at London on the same tide, within an hour-and-a-half of each other! The three—*Ariel, Taeping* and *Serica*—all broke the record for the China to London run by making it in 99 days.

The speed of those three clippers may be compared with the record of a slower ship, the misnamed *Highflyer,* built in 1861, and also in the tea trade. Her voyages from Shanghai to London required about 130 days.

Another close race was run by *Ethiopian* and *Orontes* in 1886. The two clippers departed from Sydney, Australia together and saw each other several times during their passage. *Ethiopian* won the race by docking only one tide ahead of her rival. On her first voyage, *Ethiopian* sailed from London to Melbourne in 68 days.

Many of the long voyages of the 19th Century full-rigged ships brought disaster or near-disaster in exposure to sudden squalls and gales. *Windsor Castle,* built in 1857, suffered major damage in a gale and snowstorm at Cape Horn in 1871 on her way home to England from Sydney. The mainmast crashed down, bringing with it the mizzen top and badly damaging the bulwarks on one side. Because the mast and its gear were dragging in the water, the crew was unable to steer and waves broke aboard. In great danger, the ship was saved by the heroic work of passengers and crew. The passengers manned the pumps for days while the crew cut the mainmast free and re-rigged the other two masts to permit the *Windsor Castle* to sail. The crew managed to sail to Rio de Janeiro, where the ship was put in dry dock and repaired. 269 days after leaving Sydney, Australia, she finally reached England.

One of the great mysteries associated with full-rigged ships was the tragic end of *Madagascar,* built in 1837. She vanished in 1853 somewhere in the Atlantic Ocean while hauling passengers and a cargo of gold. Some years later a woman who said she had been a nurse on the ship reported in New Zealand that the crew had killed the ship's officers in a mutiny and that the male passengers perished when the crew set fire to *Madagascar.* Young women on the ship were put in boats to be taken ashore with the gold. However, according to the nurse's story, the gold and most of the crew were lost in the surf and only the nurse and two crew members survived. One of those was later hanged for murder in San Francisco and the other could not be found. There is no proof for this story other than the word of the nurse, but there is also no evidence for doubting it.

BANGALORE

Many a Tall Ship has disappeared without a trace; in a few other cases, ships have vanished leaving at least a theory on what happened, even if there is no firm proof. An example is *Bangalore,* a full-rigged iron ship built in England in 1886. In 1908, she left Norfolk, Virginia, on her way to Honolulu with a cargo of coal for the U.S. Navy. She was seen near the Equator, but was never again reliably reported.

A former master of *Bangalore* later said he believed the ship was in a collision off Cape Horn with *Falklandbank,* another sailing vessel which also disappeared. The captain said both ships were sighted near each other in stormy weather, but he did not explain the source of his belief.

The ill-fated *Bangalore* was 260.2 feet long, had a beam of 39.9 feet and displaced 1,743 tons.

The Mariners' Museum at Newport News, Virginia has a quarter-inch model of *Bangalore* by Carroll Ray Sawyer of Manchester, New Hampshire. The museum considers it one of its best models.

HMS BEAGLE

HMS *Beagle* was built as a warship, but won world-wide fame in the peaceful pursuit of science.

In her 50-year career, starting with her launching in 1820 near London, *Beagle* made three long, significant voyages for geographical and other scientific exploration. It was the second voyage, from 1831 to 1836, for which the world remembers *Beagle* as the vehicle that carried the young naturalist, Charles Darwin. On that long voyage to the coastlines and islands of the Southern Hemisphere, Darwin collected a multitude of specimens that provided much of the information that he later synthesized into his theory of evolution.

Beagle was a 10-gun brig of 235 tons. No giant, *Beagle* was only 90 feet long on deck, but large enough to carry six boats used for exploration. She was not a rare ship—the forty-first of her class to be built—and by the time she was launched, there was no war to fight. For the first four years of her life, *Beagle* was idle. By 1825, her hull showed signs of rot. When her hull was repaired, a mizzenmast was added to her rig; then she was assigned to work as a surveying vessel. She spent four years, starting in 1826, in the difficult undertaking of charting the waters near the Straits of Magellan and Cape Horn.

During the winter of 1828 the expedition was in desperate condition. Provisions were running out, the crew was afflicted with scurvy, and the ship was suffering effects of Cape Horn's wild winter gales. The distraught captain brought the ship to a small port on the Straits of Magellan—aptly named Port Famine. When the ship was safe he went to his cabin and shot himself.

The replacement was a young captain who re-provisioned the ship and continued the work of establishing precise longitude readings and exploring. He later wrote a two-volume account of the first and second voyages.

Darwin, then 22, was taken along as a naturalist on the second voyage, which started in 1831. In South America he explored the coast, studying plants and animals, and made many journeys inland to the mountains and plains. He found fossils of seashells at high altitudes. On the Galapagos Islands he observed the mammoth tortoises and other animals and plants different from any in existence elsewhere on earth, but related, Darwin believed, to similar species he saw in Ecuador.

When *Beagle* returned to England in 1836, Darwin brought his copious notes and used them to write an account of the five-year voyage. In 1845, a revised version was published as "Voyage of the Beagle." That book brought world fame to both Darwin and *Beagle*.

In 1845, despite her newly spreading fame, *Beagle*'s sailing days came to an end. Most of her rigging was removed, and she was ignominiously reduced to serving as a warehouse. Her ungrateful government owners even changed her name to the bland *Watch Vessel 7.* Darwin published his great work, "Origin of Species," in 1859. *Beagle* was scrapped in 1870 and there are no known remains.

Beagle should have had a figurehead of the dog for which she was named, but there is no record of it.

BLUENOSE AND THEBAUD

Fishermen from Nova Scotia and New England used big schooners for fishing in those shallow waters of the sea known as the Banks, southeast of Newfoundland and Nova Scotia, and the schooners occasionally took part in organized races. The first one was in 1886 and the last in 1938. The two most famous schooners to vie against each other in these contests were *Bluenose* from the Lunenberg fleet, and *Gertrude L. Thebaud* from the Gloucester fleet.

In 1923, in the North Atlantic Fisherman Races, *Bluenose* was the winner. In 1930, they raced off Boston for the Sir Thomas Lipton Trophy and *Thebaud* won. *Bluenose* won the International Fisherman's cup Race off Halifax in 1931. Their final race was staged in 1938, but unfortunately, *Bluenose* broke a shaft in her steering soon after the start.

So the results were inconclusive. It could be argued that *Gertrude Thebaud* made the better showing, because she was 12 feet shorter and carried less canvas. Or, one could look at the record and argue that *Bluenose* won two to one among the three races completed.

COPENHAGEN

The *Copenhagen,* a five-masted bark, was built in Great Britain for a Danish firm, around 1920 to combine sail-training for future officers of the merchant marine with cargo hauling. This ship could carry 48 students in addition to a weighty cargo. She displaced 4,000 tons.

Copenhagen sailed from Buenos Aires for Melbourne on December 14, 1928, a trip not estimated to take more than 70 days, with 20 crew members and 40 cadets. She never arrived in Melbourne. Although she was equipped with the radio apparatus of her time, she was never heard from. She simply disappeared, presumably in the South Atlantic. Many nations helped conduct a wide search but no trace of the bark was ever found. It is assumed that she foundered with all hands, but what really happened to the *Copenhagen* remains one of the unsolved mysteries of the sea.

FRANCE II AND PREUSSEN

The two largest sailing vessels ever built were both European—*France II* and *Preussen.* *France II,* built in 1911 in the country whose name she bears, displaced 7,800 tons, while *Preussen,* built in 1902 in Germany, displaced 5,081 tons. The two behemoths of sail were close to each other in sparred length, with *Preussen* at 436 feet edging out *France II* at 420 feet. Their beams were about the same: 53 feet for the French ship and 52 feet for *Preussen.*

They share honors and fates. The French vessel is the record holder as the largest sailing ship ever built, while the German ship holds the record as the largest full-rigged ship ever built. In addition, *Preussen* was the only five-masted full-rigged ship. *France II* was also five-masted, but she was rigged as a bark.

The two were unquestionably big, and both got into trouble early and had short careers. The French giant of the seas lasted only 11 years before she drifted onto a coral reef in the Pacific, near Noumea at a time when there was insufficient wind to steer her. She could have been salvaged, but because of economic conditions, her owners decided to sell her for scrap.

Preussen suffered an unfortunate accident of a different sort, also not her fault. In 1910, when she was only eight years old, she was rammed hard amidships by a British vessel whose captain apparently underestimated the large ship's speed. The accident occurred in the English Channel, and *Preussen* was towed to a harbor, but was never repaired.

Both five-masters deployed vast areas of sail. *France II* flew more than 68,000 square feet—about an acre and a half, and could make 16 to 17 knots with her 32 sails. *Preussen* put up 59,000 square feet in 30 sails, and was credited with 16 knots.

As products of the 20th Century, both ships had steam power aboard, too, and therefore required small crews. Both used steam power on deck to move the heavy sails and yards. *Preussen* had an ingenious arrangement to swing the three lowest yards at the same time when the ship tacked. *France II* had four steam-powered winches to handle cargo at her four hatches. She required a crew of only 45; *Preussen* was manned by 46. Both were designed to compete on long hauls with steamships as freighters and passenger carriers.

Preussen sailed from Hamburg to a port in Chile in 57 days in 1903, setting a record.

France II could take on more than 78,000 cubic feet of water ballast when she had to sail without a cargo. She had about 30 miles of running rigging. Her mainmast was 210 feet above the waterline. *Preussen's* was even higher—225 feet.

MARY CELESTE

The fate of the brigantine *Mary Celeste* is one of the long-standing mysteries of the sea which will probably never be solved. It all started in 1872. *Mary Celeste* and another brigantine, *Dei Gratia,* from Nova Scotia, left New York 10 days apart, both headed for the Mediterranean. As *Dei Gratia* neared Gibraltar on December 4, her crew was astonished to see *Mary Celeste,* under short canvas, apparently drifting.

The captain of the *Dei Gratia,* noting that not only was she adrift, but no one was visible on deck, sent the first mate and two seamen in a small boat to check on the other ship. They found the ship was abandoned, her lifeboat was missing. Checking further, they found the ship was in seaworthy condition, and her log had no entries after November 24—ten days before the crew from *Dei Gratia* came aboard.

Everything was not shipshape on board *Mary Celeste,* but there were no signs of violence or struggle or any clear indication of what would make her crew abandon the ship. Her cargo, barrels of alcohol, was slightly damaged. The binnacle was out of place and broken. The chronometer and sextant were missing. There was still food and drink among the ship's supplies. There was some sea water in the hold, but not a dangerous amount.

The Nova Scotians of the *Dei Gratia* decided to sail *Mary Celeste* to Gibraltar, where an official inquiry was conducted. An investigator found stains, but analysis determined that they were not blood. The investigation resulted in no answer to the questions that have persisted ever since: Why was the ship abandoned?

What happened to the crew?

THOMAS W. LAWSON

At the beginning of the 20th Century, schooners found profitable work in hauling coal. More than 50 five-masted schooners were built as coal ships, and 10 six-masted schooners were built in the early 1900's. The *Thomas W. Lawson,* launched at Quincy, Mass., in 1902, went them one better; she actually had seven masts. As was usual with schooners with three or more masts, all were the same height and all were gaff-rigged with topsails.

The steel-hulled *Lawson* was a record breaker; she was the only seven-master ever built. She was 395 feet in overall length—extremely long, but not so long as a few ships built later. She could haul 9,000 tons of coal.

After working four years at the job for which she was built, *Lawson* switched fuels, becoming an oil tanker under sail—a rare status. In 1907, only five years after she first sailed, *Lawson* suffered an ignominious accident. While anchored in the Scilly Isles, off England's southwest coast, she was hit by a gale and driven onto a reef, where she sank.

PAMIR

One of the last steel-hulled four-masted ships ever built, *Pamir* was launched in 1921, at a time when steamships were dominating the ocean freight business. She was a bark 422 feet long and therefore in a class with those giant five-masters, *France II* and *Preussen,* which were also built in this century. *Pamir* displaced 4,670 tons—considerably less than the others.

While the other two had short lives due to misfortune, *Pamir* worked for more than 30 years as a cargo vessel. In the early part of her career, she sailed to Chile for nitrates; later, she hauled freight between Europe and Australia.

Pamir was built for the German shipping firm of F. Laeisz, whose vessels all had names starting with the letter P. *Preussen* was one. Another is *Peking,* which survives today and is a prime attraction at South Street Seaport in New York City. Laeisz called his ships the Flying P Line of Hamburg.

In 1950, *Pamir* was abondoned in Antwerp, Belgium. The German government bought her and converted her to new use as a training ship, after installing an auxiliary engine. She was again being used as a cargo vessel and was carrying grain in 1957, when she was struck by a hurricane in the Atlantic Ocean. *Pamir* was blown over and she sank with her crew of 80—joining the hundreds and hundreds of sailing ships that lost their duels with storms at sea.

Glossary

Aback A square sail is *aback* when the wind is on the side of the sail that will drive the vessel astern.

Abeam At right angles to the keel.

Aft Toward the stern; same as *abaft*.

Alee Away from the direction of the wind. When the wheel of a vessel sailing close-hauled is turned "*hard alee*" or "*helm's alee*," the ship turns to the other tack.

Aloft Above the deck.

Amidships Toward the center of the vessel.

Anchor A device to grip the bottom and hold a vessel by the attached rope or chain.

Anchor's aweigh The anchor is off the bottom.

Anemometer An instrument to measure wind velocity.

Astern Behind the ship; backwards.

Athwart Across the width of the vessel; at right angle to the fore-and-aft line.

Back The wind *backs* when it changes in a counter-clockwise direction.

Backstay A part of the standing rigging supporting the mast from aft.

Baldheaded schooner One without topmasts.

Ballast Any heavy material, such as stone, iron or lead, placed in the lower part of a sailing vessel, or attached to its keel, to increase stability by lowering the center of gravity.

Bank A relatively shallow area such as the Grand Banks in the Atlantic Ocean near Newfoundland.

Bark A sailing vessel with three or more masts, square-rigged on all but the aftermost mast, which is fore-and-aft rigged.

Barkentine A vessel of three or more masts, square rigged on the foremast only, fore-and-aft rigged on the others.

Barometer An instrument for measuring atmospheric pressure.

Barrel-bowed Nearly circular at the deckline of the bow.

Beam The greatest width of a vessel. Also, a thwartship timber supporting the deck.

Beam wind One that blows across the ship at right angle to the fore-and-aft line. A ship sailing with a beam wind is on a *beam reach*.

Beating Sailing to windward.

Becket A looped rope, strap or *grommet* used to hold ropes, spars or oars in proper position.

Before the mast The sailors living in the *forecastle* are before the mast.

Before the wind Sailing in the same direction as the wind. Also called running.

Belay To make fast; stop.

Belaying pin A rod of wood or metal used for securing the running rigging.

Below Beneath the deck.

Bend To attach a sail to a spar. Also, a knot fastening one line to another.

Bilge The lowest part of the vessel's interiors, where water collects.

Binnacle A box or stand for the compass, usually with lights.

Block A ship's pulley, consisting of a frame supporting a sheave or roller, over which the lines are run.

Bluff When applied to the shape of a hull, full at the bow.

Boat A vessel of indefinite size, usually a small vessel carried aboard a ship.

Bobstay Chain or wire from the bowsprit to the stem to support the bowsprit and counteract the pulling force of the stays.

Boom The spar to which the foot of a fore-and-aft sail is connected.

Bow The forward part of a vessel; opposite of *stern*.

Bowsprit A spar projecting forward from the bow.

Brace On square-rigged ships, a line leading aft from the end of a yard. Yards are *braced-in* when they are pulled athwartships.

Brig A sailing ship with two masts, square-rigged on both.

Brigantine A two-masted sailing vessel, square rigged on the foremast only.

Brightwork Brass kept polished or wood kept varnished.

Bulkhead Partition inside a vessel.

Bulwarks Built-up sides above the deck of a vessel.

Bumpkin A projecting strut at deck level at the stern.

Buntline Ropes fastened to the foot of a square sail for use in furling.

Buoy An anchored float, including those used as aids to navigation.

Cap A piece of wood or metal at the joint between two sections of mast. Part fits over the head of the lower mast; the upper mast fits through a hole in another part.

Capstan A cylinder with long removable arms used to apply leverage in raising an anchor or sails. On modern yachts, *winches* do similar work.

Carronade A short cannon of the 18th and 19th Centuries.

Carvel-built Smooth-sided. Planking edge to edge rather than overlapped.

Cat boat Sailboat with one mast, at the bow.

Cat Head A heavy timber projecting outboard horizontally near the bow for use in retrieving the anchor, a process called *catting the anchor*.

Caulk To force material such as *oakum* into the seams between planking to prevent leaking.

"Charlie Noble" The nickname for the galley smokepipe.

Chart A map for navigation.

Chine Where the topsides meet the bottom, forming an edge in hulls not rounded.

Clew Lower corners of a square sail. Aft lower corner of a fore-and-aft sail.

Clinker-built Construction method in which planks overlap. *Lapstrake* construction.

Close-hauled Sailing as close into the wind as possible.

Club A short spar at the foot of a fore-and-aft sail.

Coaming Raised edge around hatches, other deck openings and doors to prevent water from entering.

Corvette An armed vessel with guns along one deck only. Also called *sloop of war*.

Course In square-rigged vessels, the largest sail, set on the lower yard. Also, the direction sailed is the *compass course*.

Crance A metal band on the bowsprit with an eye for the bobstay. Also called cranze iron.

Cringle A ring sewn into a sail, for attaching a line.

Cutter A single-masted sailing vessel with two or more sails before the mast. Also, a seaworthy patrol vessel, as a Coast Guard cutter.

Dead-eye A round block of wood with three or four holes, through which lines are passed to tighten the standing rigging. Used before *turnbuckles*.

Deadrise The angle at which the bottom of a vessel rises toward the topsides. A flat-bottomed vessel has no deadrise; a V-bottomed one has.

Eye A ring through which a line is passed.

Fathom Six feet or 1.83 meters. Used in reporting depth of water.

Flare In describing shapes of ships, the outward slope of the sides. Also, a distress signal emitting smoke or light.

Flemish horse A short footrope.

Foot Bottom edge of a sail.

Footrope A rope suspended a few feet below a yard, bowsprit or spanker boom, to stand on while handling sails.

Fore-and-aft Along the vessel's length rather than athwart.

Forecastle On a ship, the forward part of the interior, between foremast and bow. (Pronounced fo'c's'le)

Foremast The mast nearest the bow, in all ships having two or more masts.

Founder To fill with water and sink.

Freeboard Distance between the deck and the waterline.

Frigate A warship of the 18th and early 19th Centuries.

Full-rigged ship Has three masts, all with square sails.

Furl To roll or bunch up a sail and secure it to a yard or boom.

Futtock A piece of wood shaped to be joined with other such pieces to form a frame for a vessel.

Futtock Plate The platform of a top.

Futtock Shrouds Iron rods supporting the futtock plate and topmast rigging.

Gaff A spar on which the head of a four-sided fore-and-aft rigged sail is set. The gaff pivots on the mast, which it meets at an angle.

Galleass A warship used in the Mediterranean from the 15th to the 18th Centuries, lateen-rigged on three masts.

Galleon A sailing vessel of the 15th to 17th Centuries, used in commerce and war.

Galley A seagoing vessel propelled by oars, sometimes aided by sails. Also, the ship's kitchen.

Gammon Iron A collar to secure the bowsprit.

Gangway A passage way on a ship or a ladder up its side.

Garboard strake The planking next to the keel.

Gob Line A support for a martingale.

Gooseneck A device for securing a boom to a mast while allowing the boom to move.

Gunwale The rail of a vessel. (Pronounced "gunnel")

Guy A horizontal or inclined support. A vertical support is a stay.

Halyards Lines or wires used to pull up sails or yards.

Hard alee A skipper's command when coming about. See "alee."

Hawse Pipes Holes through which the anchor chain passes.

Head Upper corner of a three or four-sided sail. Also, a ship's lavatory.

Headsails All sails forward of the foremast. Includes jibs and staysails.

Heave To throw by hand, as in heaving a line.

Heave to To arrange sails and helm so that a ship will head up out of the trough of waves, without requiring constant attention at the helm. A technique for riding out a storm.

Heel To tilt.

Helm The tiller or wheel controlling the rudder.

Hog Said of a vessel's hull when it droops at its ends.

Hold The main cargo space in a vessel.

Hulk A wrecked or stripped hull, including one used as a warehouse.

Jackstay An iron rod at the top of a yard.

Jack-yards Short spars attached to the top of a mast and the end of a gaff to support a jack-yard topsail, a triangular sail.

Jeer A heavy block and tackle for hoisting heavy yards.

Jib A triangular sail set at or near the bow or on the bowsprit. If there are two such sails, the one further forward is the jib and the other is usually called a *staysail*. When there are more than two, terms such as *inner* and *outer jib* and *flying jib* are used.

Jib Boom A spar mounted on the bowsprit.

Jibe To change the direction of a sailing vessel by turning the stern across the wind direction. In a square-rigger, to *wear*.

Jib-headed topsail A triangular sail set between the gaff and the topmast without jack-yards.

Jiggermast The aft mast on some vessels with two or more masts, a yawl or ketch. It carries the jigger, a small triangular sail on the stern.

Jumper A chain from the forward end of the jib boom to the lower end of the martingale.

Jury Rig A temporary mast and spars set up when others have been damaged.

Keel The vessel's backbone from which frames rise like ribs.

Ketch A two-masted vessel with foremast the taller and mizzen forward of the rudderpost.

Knot A measure of speed. One knot is one nautical mile per hour.

Ladder A ship's stairs.

Lateen A triangular sail on a long yard set at an angle of about 45 degrees to the deck.

Lanyard A rope reeved through the deadeye to tighten the rigging. Or, a line used to make anything fast—even a short line to secure a knife.

Lapstrake A method of boatbuilding in which the planks overlap. See *clinker*.

Latitude Distance north or south of the equator, expressed in degrees.

Lead A piece of lead on a line for measuring the depth of the water. "Heave the lead" means to take a sounding, to measure the depth.

Lee The side of a vessel away from the direction in which the wind is blowing. Also, *leeward*.

Leech The aft edge of a triangular sail, or side of a square sail. Also spelled *leach*.

Lee Shore Shore with the wind blowing toward it; the shore that lies leeward of the vessel.

Letter of marque License granted to a privateer to plunder enemy commerce.

Longitude Distance east or west of the meridian through Greenwich, England.

Loose-footed sail A sail whose foot is not attached to a boom all along its length.

Luff The forward edge of fore-and-aft sail. As a verb, to bring the vessel too close to the wind, so that the sails shake.

Mainmast The highest mast on a vessel or the center mast on a three-masted vessel.

Mainsail Largest sail on mainmast.

Main Royal Fifth level sail, below skysail.

Manrope A safety rope at the side of a ladder or gangway.

Martingale A short spar pointing down beneath the bowsprit. Also called *dolphin striker*.

Martnets Leechlines on a square sail.

Mizzen On a three-masted vessel, the aftermost mast. On a ketch or yawl, the aft mast or sail.

Moon-Raker In old sailing ships, a small sail set above the skysail. Also called *Moon-sail*.

Nautical Mile 1852 meters or 6,076.1 feet; about 1.15 statute miles.

Oakum Fiber from old ropes used for caulking.

Off Soundings In water more than 100 fathoms deep.

Orlop Deck The lowest deck.

Overall Length In legal terms, the length of a vessel from tip of the stem to the aftmost part of the stern. In this book, sparred length.

Parcel To wind strips of canvas tightly around wire or rope as part of the process of worming, parceling and serving.

Parrel A sliding collar of rope, metal or wood, holding a yard to the mast without allowing vertical movement.

Peak Upper and outer corner of a gaff-rigged fore-and-aft sail.

Pink or Pinky A vessel with a narrow "pinked," overhanging stern.

Pinnace 17th Century three-masted square-rigger.

Point One of 32 points of the compass. 11¼ degrees. As a verb, to sail close to the wind.

Poop A raised deck at the stern of a vessel.

Pooped A vessel is pooped when a following sea breaks over the stern.

Port Left side.

Privateer A vessel commissioned to prey on enemy commerce.

Quarter Aft side, as in port quarter.

Raffee A triangular topsail set from the truck and yardarms of the highest yard. Also moon-raker.

Rail The top of the bulwarks.

Raise To "raise a light" is to see it.

Rake Angle. A raked mast slopes aft.

Ratlines Rope rungs seized to the shrouds, forming a ladder for climbing aloft. (Pronounced "ratlins")

Ready about Preparatory command before "Hard alee" or "Helm's alee" in tacking.

Reef To reduce exposed sail area.

Reef points Lines placed in a series parallel to a boom or yard for fastening a reefed sail.

Rig The arrangement of a vessel's masts and sails.

Rigging All the lines and their fittings on a vessel. The standing rigging supports the mast or masts. The running rigging raises, lowers and controls the sails.

Robands Small lines used to tie a square sail to a jackstay.

Royal On a square-rigged vessel, the sail above the topgallant sail.

Schooner A fore-and-aft rigged vessel, with two or more masts, the last carrying the mainsail.

Serving Winding thin line, such as *marline* (called *small stuff*) tightly around a rope or wire. Often done with the aid of a *serving mallet,* a simple device for pulling the line tight.

Sheer The line, usually curved, of a vessel's side from fore to aft.

Sheet A line used to control the position of a sail.

Ship A full-rigged ship or ship-rigged vessel to some. More generally, any vessel.

Shipwright A skilled builder of vessels.

Shrouds Lines or wires from the masthead to the side of the vessel to support the mast as part of the standing rigging.

Skipper Master of a vessel, especially a yacht.

Skysail A light sail above the royal on a square-rigged vessel.

Sloop A single-masted sailing vessel with one headsail.

Sound To measure the depth of water.

Spanker A gaff-rigged fore-and-aft sail at the stern of a bark or a full-rigged ship.

Spar A mast, boom, yard or other support for sails, originally of wood.

Spinnaker A large, lightweight three-cornered sail set on the foremast for sailing downwind.

Spritsail A four-sided sail stretched by a spar called the *sprit,* extending from the peak diagonally to the mast near the deck.

Squaresail A four-sided sail hung from a spar called a yard.

Starboard Right side.

Stay A line or wire supporting a mast from its front (forestay) or back (backstay).

Staysail A sail set on a stay.

Stem The fore part of a vessel's bow joining the keel.

Stern The after part of a vessel.

Sterncastle The high portion of the stern of medieval ships.

Strakes Planks of a vessel's side, running along its depth.

Strike To lower sail, yard or mast.

Studding Sail Light extra sails, used on square-rigged vessels sailing downwind, set on spars rigged out from the yards.

Tack The lower forward corner of a fore-and-aft sail. Also, to change direction of a sailing vessel by turning the bow across the wind direction. See *jibe,* the opposite maneuver.

Taffrail A rail at the stern.

Tiller A horizontal bar, usually of wood, to control the rudder, for steering.

Top A platform on a mast, supported by trestle trees.

Topgallant Mast In square-rigged vessels, the third section of a mast, above the topmast, which is the second section. The first is the lower mast.

Topsails Second and third level sails.

Transom A flat vertical stern.

Treenails Wooden pins or dowels used to attach planks to timbers in wooden vessels. (Pronounced "trunnels")

Trestle-trees Two short timbers attached to a mast in fore and aft position, to support a top.

Truck A disc at the head of a mast to which halyards are attached.

Try Works Equipment for cooking and rendering blubber on a whaling ship.

Tumble Home The inward curve of the topsides of a hull.

Veer When the wind changes direction clockwise, it veers. Opposite of *back.*

Wear To change direction of a vessel by moving the stern, rather than the bow, across the wind. Opposite of *tack.* Square-riggers *wear;* fore-and-aft vessels executing the same maneuver *jibe.*

Weigh To weigh anchor is to raise it.

Wind Air in motion. Wind direction is expressed as where the wind is blowing from.

Windjammer A sailing vessel, especially a large one, carrying passengers.

Windlass A winch operated by hand (with a crank) or by power, for raising an anchor.

Windward The direction from which the wind is blowing. Opposite of *leeward.*

Worm To wind thin line (small stuff) between the strands of a rope.

Yard A spar from which a square sail is hung.

Yard-arm The end of a yard.

Yawl A two-masted sailing vessel with the mizzen or jigger—mast shorter than the foremast and set aft of the rudderpost.

Yawl Boat A powerful small workboat often carried on davits at the stern of a schooner or other vessel sailing without an auxiliary engine.